DUNDEE FROM THE TRAM CARS.

THE DEN AND CASTLE OF MAINS.

DUNDEE

FROM THE TRAM CARS.

An Illustrated Guide to the City and its Surroundings.

WRITTEN BY ALAN REID, F.S.A., SCOT.

DUNDEE:

PRINTED FOR THE TRAMWAY COMMITTEE.

BURNS & HARRIS, 112 NETHERGATE.

1912.

TRAMWAYS COMMITTEE.

—o—

Lord Provost Urquhart.

A. Spence.

D. Neave.

R. L. B. Watt.

J. M. Nairn.

W. Forwell.

Rev. Dr. Walsh.

Walker S. Melville.

W. H. Buist.

G. A. Johnston, *Convener*.

INTRODUCTORY.

—◦≡|·|≡◦—

THE City of Dundee, its suburbs, and dependencies, are served by nearly thirty miles of Tramways. The Horse and Steam haulage of other days has given place to Electric Traction ; the cars are of the newest description ; the service is rapid, frequent, and accurate ; and the staff a model of ability and courtesy. Over 26,000 miles are covered weekly, representing the conveyance of over seventeen million passengers annually, the traffic receipts reaching the respectable annual figure of Sixty-three Thousand Pounds. A committee of the City Council is responsible for the administration of this important branch of public service, whose immediate oversight is under guidance of which it would be difficult to speak too highly.

The Service gives direct and speedy access to almost every populous district of the City, and leads to its suburbs and outskirts by the shortest routes available. In the pages that follow, an effort has been made to induce the citizens, who may not be aware of the beautiful surroundings of Dundee, to make closer acquaintance with them, and thus enjoy the benefits of health and beauty brought within their easy reach by the Tram Car service. The *guide* aims at conciseness of statement, and suggestions of such objective points and circular journeys as will delight and refresh the toiler who spends an evening or an afternoon in exploring the lovely districts that surround the City of the Tay.

ILLUSTRATIONS.

CONTENTS.

—◆●◆—

NOTE.

The line Drawings, illustrating several interesting details noted in the text, were specially prepared by Mr Joseph Lee. Acknowledgement should also be made of Mr Frank Sharp's kindness in placing at my disposal his interesting series of Photographs of Dundee and district.   A. R.

LORD PROVOST URQUHART.

THE TOWN HOUSE.   MARKET DAY IN HIGH STREET.

Dundee from the Tram Cars.

I.—The Perth Road Section.

IT was a feather in the cap of " Bonnie Dundee ' when William Adams was retained as the Architect of the Town House. No other Scottish Burgh, not even the Metropolis, could boast of Municipal Buildings designed by an architect so distinguished. But the Tayside city is nothing if not enterprising ; and it seems quite natural to find the spirit of Progress thus active about the middle of the 19th Century.

The Pillars ! What a wealth of significance that old title has for the true Dundonian ! The Adams Piazza has been the trysting place of many generations, and still it is, as it will remain the heart of Dundee's social well-being. Round the Pillars surge the tides of its Commerce ; from the Pillars radiate its busiest avenues. It was peculiarly fitting that its splendid Tramway System should focus itself upon this centre ; that its beneficent service should spring near this fount of human inspiration. Despite its name and fame as a bustling mart of Commerce ; despite the narrowness and crookedness of its older streets ; the ancient city has points of beauty and interest all its own. Here a clearance has been made, and there a broadening of the bounds, but the relics of history are numerous still, and many objects are left to recall the story of the eventful past. Here a palace rears its stately head, there a spacious thoroughfare attracts the eye; but St. Mary's ancient Tower, and the narrow Overgate still have their power to charm, perhaps, as never before. The blend of Old and New is perfect, the contrasts striking, the *ensemble* grand. *Without* its picturesque surroundings, its magnificent approaches, and its modern developments, Dundee is genuinely attractive, pictorially and historically. When these inherent qualities are reinforced by the charms of the Tay, the noble Law, bonnie Balgay, and the Baxter Park, as by a flawless environment of sylvan beauty, admiration *must* be whole-hearted to be appropriate or sincere.

The Tramways open out these points of beauty and interest as nothing else can. All the routes lead directly from the heart of the city to some rural terminus, where nature smiles in her every guise and mood. How many among the toiling thousands know these charms? Conveyance within the City is good, a necessity of the times indeed; but to be carried from its din and bustle, to leave behind its smoke and dust, to be free, even for a short time, from its cares and worries is, surely, infinitely better? Out to pleasant Invergowrie and the banks of Tay; across to Lochee and the breezes of the Law; over by Downfield or Clepington to the classic joys of Mains; down by Broughty to Monifieth, with the golden fringes of Fife for company; why! there is magic in the very thought, and the civic heart should rejoice in its attainment, now so easy, and so cheap. The *seeing eye* adds amazingly to the delight of even a Tramway journey. Let us employ it as we leave the High Street *en route* for Invergowrie and the terminus at Ninewells. This is the Perth Road section of the System, and runs a distance of two and a half miles. As the car sweeps into the Nethergate, we may glance at the ancient turreted

CONVENER JOHNSTON.

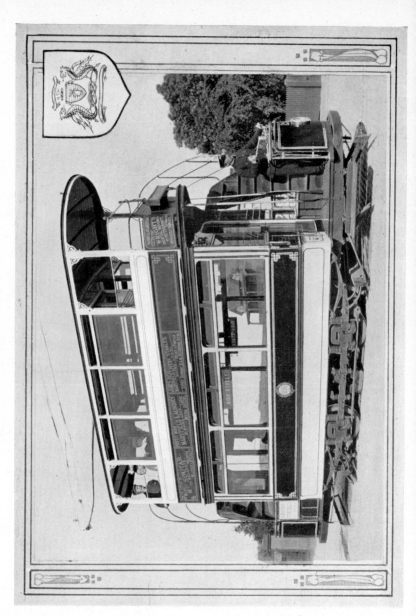

mansion that fills the space between the Overgate and the route by which we travel. It is interesting to know that within these walls, Anne, who became Duchess of Monmouth, was born in 1650; and that, a year later, they sheltered General Monk, whose memory was long execrated in Dundee on account of the cruelties attendant on its capture by his English soldiery.

Southwards, Whitehall Street recalls to memory the fact that a royal residence once occupied the site of this imposing thoroughfare. It is on record that Mary, Queen of Scots, with Lord Darnley, sojourned for a week within Whitehall, and that her son. James VI., often resided within this ancient palace of the Stuarts. The Gilfillan Memorial Hall and Church closes the vista of the handsome street. George Gilfillan, as a pulpit orator, and *litterateur*, was a credit to his country and an honour to Dundee, which will not readily forget his genius and character. The ministry of his successor, Rev. David Macrae, within the memorial buildings was, also, a notable feature in the city's ecclesiastical experience.

On the same side is Union Street, with the Royal Hotel in which is incorporated the old Thistle Hall, now a magnificent Dining Saloon. This important avenue gives direct access to the Caledonian and Tay Bridge Stations, the Tay Ferries, and the Esplanade, one of the finest sea promenades in the country. But the City Churches, opposite, claim our more undivided attention. There, rising in impressive dignity over the ancient cross, and the comparatively modern East, West, and Middle Churches, is the "Auld Steeple," the dominating feature of every Dundee landscape, and the dearest object to the heart of every patriotic native of the good old town.

The Dundonian may well be pardoned for his pride in this noble relic of the past. Not only is it beautiful as an

THE MERCAT CROSS.

architectural triumph, and without a peer among British towers, it is a tangible record of all that has gone to make Dundee historically eminent. It has played many parts in the life of the city, and has been a belfry, prison, fortress, or sanctuary as was necessary or inevitable. Tradition associates the revolt of the patriotic Wallace with the ancient tower of St. Mary's; the defenders of Dundee made their last stand against Monk within its sturdy walls; and under its shadow the General Assembly of the Kirk of Scotland was convened by King James in 1597.

The future safety of this venerable structure was assured through the public spirit of the citizens some thirty years ago. Sir Gilbert Scott was responsible for the skilful restoration then effected, and it speaks well for the insight and foresight of those to whom the very dust of the fabric was dear, that the praises of this great authority on Gothic Architecture exceeded even the eulogiums of its active local admirers. In his Report to them, Sir Gilbert averred:—"It is not only one of the noblest towers in Great Britain, but the originality of its design, and the bold simplicity of its entire ideal, united with its wonderful effectiveness, give it a very high rank among the works of our great mediæval architects "

That, surely, should satisfy the most exacting, and cause many to take a renewed interest in this magnificent remnant of 15th century architecture. It is now a show place and a museum, from whose lofty battlements, 160 feet in air, may be viewed the finest panorama of urban, suburban, and marine scenery which the district has to offer.

Westwards, once more, we soon reach St. Paul's U.F. Church, a fine steepled building, erected some ten years after the Disruption, and for long regarded as one of the leading churches in the denomination. It knew the ministry of men like Dr. William Wilson, Richard Watterston, and Principal Patrick, and has always been notable for the liberality of its members, and the excellence of its congregational praise.   St. Enoch's Established Church, which marks the ancient city boundary, stands nearly opposite.   The secession of the Rev. Wm. Knight, latterly of the St. Andrews professorial body, gave this church much prominence at a critical stage in its history.   St. Andrews R.C. Church, the pro-Cathedral of the diocese, and the spacious Queen's Hotel, are also prominent objects of the locality.   Morgan Castle, another relic of old Dundee, in one of the rooms of which Sir William Allan, M.P., the engineer poet, was born, the Harris Academy, and the University College come rapidly under review.   Assuredly there is no lack of interest here, nor elsewhere on this fascinating route.

This youngest of Scottish Colleges originated in the magnificent bequests made to the City by certain members of the Baxter family. The College buildings which were simply the West end residences of a few wealthy Dundonians, are unpretentious in the extreme, and give but little indication of the important work performed within them. Recently, the Medical School has been accommodated in admirable permanent quarters; and in due time the other Faculties will flourish within an edifice worthy of the fine site, and of the ancient University of St. Andrews with which the College is affiliated.

M'CHEYNE'S TOMB, ST. PETER'S CHURCH.

Among the older buildings displaced by the new College was the Disruption building known as St. John's Free Church. Its congregation now assemble within the handsome structure which marks the commencement of Perth Road proper, and whose lofty spire seems to dominate the galaxy of fine churches in the neighbourhood. St. Mark's, Ryehill, and the M'Cheyne Memorial are numbered among these, but in interest they are all eclipsed by the plain, almost unadorned bulk of St. Peter's, sacred, while it stands, as the scene of the ministry of Robert Murray M'Cheyne. This celebrated divine and writer, whose fame is preserved in the Scottish classic written by his friend, Dr. Andrew Bonar, enjoys a reputation that seems unaffected by the lapse of time. His saintly character and pulpit gifts made this old church a sort of rallying point for the religious fervour of the shire, and his tomb in the quiet churchyard was for long venerated as one of Scotland's holiest shrines.

But we move onwards, past the residences of merchant princes, the ever widening areas near Magdalen Green, the frequent glimpses of the famous Bridge of Tay, the Western Cemetery with its ornate and effective entrances, on to the Terminus at Ninewells, and the delights of the open country. Soon the old village of Invergowrie attracts the attention of the wanderer. The subjects of the local prophecy, attributed to Thomas the Rhymer :—

> "When the Yowes o' Gowrie come to land
> The day o' Judgment's near at hand."

THE YOWES O' GOWRIE.

are often sought in vain. The truth is, that railway operations have *landed* them long ago, and still the world wags on. The Paddock Stane legend is probably just as authentic as the other. However, the very stone by which the Deil attempted to annihilate the church of Boniface lies within the grounds of Graystane House, and not far from it is one of those pre-historic circles of standing stones so dear to the antiquary.

THE OLD STEEPLE.

THE PADDOCK, OR DEIL'S STANE, INVERGOWRIE.

The gates of Graystane Avenue are also of outstanding interest.

ENTRANCE GATE TO GRAYSTANE.

They at one time graced the enclosure round St. Paul's

Cathedral, London, and were known as the Royal gates. When the west part of the Cathedral, facing Ludgate Hill, was opened up by the removal of the railings, the late Mr Watson of Bullionfield purchased these interesting relics and had them erected here.

The ancient Church of Invergowrie, one of the oldest of Scottish stone buildings, is worth going far to see. Ivy-clad, picturesque, historic, it is in its way the 'lion' of a district whose charms are varied and numerous The great paper works at Bullionfield, and the celebrated stone quarries at Kingoodie also deserve attention. Dundee may be said to owe its being to Kingoodie, even as does the Bell Rock Light-house, which was fashioned from its stones. Assuredly, there is much to interest, instruct, and elevate in this fair portion of the City's environment.

II.—Seagate and Ferry Road Section.

Before resuming our journeying from the High Street, the neighbourhood may be accorded a share of our observation. Proceeding by Crichton Street, in the direction of the Docks, we face the Royal Arch, a splendid Gothic structure which serves as an entrance to the Western Docks. It was erected to commemorate the first visit of Queen Victoria and her consort in 1844. Its designer was the late J. T. Rochead, whose fame rests mainly on the National Monument to Wallace erected on the Abbey Craig at Stirling. The Docks are in themselves a never-failing source of attraction, and Dock Street is distinguished by several fine buildings, among them being the dignified Custom House, whose classic outlines contrast well with its naval surroundings. The air of bustle and business when the great Docks are full of craft discharging and replenishing their cargoes is indescribable. Dundee is one of our leading Scottish seaports, and an outlet for the produce of the world, whether it be jute from India, coals from England, or oil from Labrador !

Prior to the recent extension of the eastward route, the Terminus of the Tramway line was at Craigie Terrace on the Broughty Ferry Road. The new Broughty and Monifieth section is worked from that point by the District Tramway Company, but the service is continuous from the High Street to the rising golfing and seaside resort. The cars start from Castle Street, a name reminiscent of those olden days when the castles of Broughty and Dundee guarded the open shores of Tay. On the right rises the lofty spire of St. Paul's Episcopal Church, the cathedral of the diocese of Brechin, and associated with the name and memory of the "Angel Bishop" Forbes. Sir Gilbert Scott was the architect of this noble gothic fane, whose fair proportions are, unfortunately, minimised through its cramped, corner situation. A little further eastwards the Theatre and Opera House is passed, and now the route runs through a veritable labyrinth of business premises. It is interesting to observe the admirable architectural effects that are being introduced into these warehouses and offices, and it should not be forgot that though utilitarian in the mass, they represent much of the commerce which is the mainstay of the City, and, approximately, much of the wealth of the citizens.

The commercial Seagate merges into Blackscroft, a district which retains some traces of its old suburban character ; and at the City Gasworks we exchange the busier streets for the wider spaces of the Ferry Road. Passing the Cattle Market and the spacious Abbatoirs, we see to the left and right the estates and mansions of past generations of Dundee magnates, still bravely flaunting their wealth of verdure, but showing the stress of a growing City, and gracefully resigning their

INVERGOWRIE OLD CHURCH.

W. BLYTH MARTIN, TOWN CLERK.

THE ROYAL ARCH.

ancient state to the inevitable. On the right, and opposite
Craigie Terrace, is the Orphan Institution, for many years one
of the City's most useful charities, beyond and beneath it lying
the great Eastern Wharves, the Shipbuilding Yards, and the
spacious foreshore redeemed in recent years from the broad
waters of the Tay.

We are again within the domain of nature, and in full
view of the great estuary of the Tay. Lovely woodland
glimpses charm the eye as we sweep along by the old estate of
Craigie, and note in passing the charming villas springing up
on every side. The Castle of Claypotts now shows its walls
and crowsteps through the trees on the left, tempting the
digression made by many to their delight and edification. It

CLAYPOTTS CASTLE.

is not everywhere that one can see a 16th century castle roofed
and entire, or a residence built so strongly, and on such a
remarkable plan. In all probability, it was at one time
occupied by John Graham of Claverhouse, the "Bonnie
Dundee" of song and story, and thus has an additional interest
for the enlightened visitor. The association of Claypotts with
the name of Cardinal Beaton is mythical, for the crafty prelate

was safe from troubling before the date of its erection by the Strachan family.

The West Ferry, with its miles of elegant residences, castles, towers, and gardens, forms a striking object lesson on the material prosperity of the great commercial centre at whose fiat it arose, and whose minister it is. The East Ferry —Broughty Ferry proper—rose under the ægis of the Grays, whose 15th century fortress still commands the entrances of Tay. Broughty Castle, the centre of the ancient *Burgh o' Tay*, is now a government military station, and is still a picturesque object despite its modern air. Its walls stand straight and strong for all their weight of years, and bear but little trace of the many sieges they withstood throughout the troublous Stuart times. Scarcely anywhere are fairer prospects to be seen than those in which this sturdy veteran forms the predominating feature; but Broughty is beautiful both from land and sea, and its opulence is overwhelming.

The lately opened Orchar Park, and the charming Reres Hill, now alternate with the sandy beach as a rendezvous for the summer visitor. The Ferry may be regarded as the Brighton of the Tay, and surely there are few, if any, in Dundee who have not made acquaintance with its attractions. Beyond the bounds lies the modern villa-village of Barnhill, the historic estate of Grange Durham occupying the braeside rising near. Seaward, the eye roves over a wide expanse of sandy dunes to the white towers of Buddon, and soon we run within the streets of Monifieth The growth of this popular resort has been phenomenal, but is easily explained by its situation and its salubrity. They are not far wrong, perhaps, who to these inducements add its breezy, spreading links, and its splendid golf course, one of the finest sporting grounds in the Kingdom.

III.—The Lochee Section.

Sometimes, when in a jocular mood, the Lochee man, with affected gravity, will discuss with the Dundonian—Whether Lochee is a suburb of Dundee, or Dundee a suburb of Lochee? Of course, he settles the question easily, and in favour of his own town. Moreover, he never forgets to rub well in to his opponent the fact that Lochee owns a chimney, tall enough, and big enough, to make the city of chimneys turn green with envy. But, *en route* for Lochee and the Law, we shall steer clear of all local controversy, and simply accept the premier Scottish chimney as chief among the sights of the busy inland town.

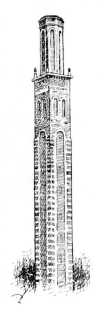

THE LOCHEE CHIMNEY.

We start from Reform Street, a finely built thoroughfare, whose vistas are closed to the South by the High Street, and the Town House, and to the North by Albert Square and the High School. Bank Street, which opens westwards from our course, deserves a word and a note in passing. Dundee's principal public room, the Kinnaird Hall is here; and facing it, the extensive printing and publishing premises founded by the late Sir John Leng, M.P. The *Dundee Advertiser* is a power among Scottish Newspapers; the *People's Journal* has grown venerable as a tribune of the working classes; and the *People's Friend* has for long been their literary guide and library. Dundee has been a pioneer in such enterprises, and leads the way in all that is of good repute in cheap periodical literature.

Lamb's Hotel, whose corner we must round, suggests popular local reminiscences of its far-seeing founder who raised it from very small beginnings to be one of the first Temperance Hotels in the Kingdom. But, meantime, the palatial structure of the Albert Institute claims our attention. This memorial to Prince Albert, filling the centre of the Square, combines a splendid Art Gallery and Museum, with an extensive Public Library and Reading Room, all remarkably well equipped, and free to the citizens, who take large advantage of their benefits. No memorial of the enlightened Prince Consort could be more appropriate to his character, and no collection of the treasures of art and literature could find worthier lodgment than in the handsome rooms of this Gothic masterpiece designed by the great Sir Gilbert Scott.

Before the western *facade*, and to right and left of the elaborate fountain, are fine statues of Robert Burns the National Poet, and of George Kinloch, M.P., celebrated as a Parliamentary Reformer. The opinions and fiery words of the laird of Kinloch, however acceptable in his constituency, were so abhorent to the Government of his time, that they locked him up in the State Prison of Edinburgh Castle. As is recorded, "Geordie" was the last tenant of that historic cell. The good Queen Victoria, and the celebrated engineer, James Carmichael, are also commemorated by bronze statues on whose merits there is occasional divergence of opinion. On the whole, however, the Albert Square statuary has meritorious qualities, and is very effectively disposed within the verge of foliage surrounding the Institute.

Chief among the other ornaments of the Albert Square is the High School, a noble building in the Grecian Style, with a central portico reminiscent of the Athenian Parthenon The adjoining High School for girls, one of the Harris benefactions, is also worthy of remark among a group of buildings of such importance as the Royal Exchange and the Eastern Club. Dundee is highly favoured educationally, and is thoroughly "up-to-date" in men, methods and machinery.

The lofty range of modern Buildings from which the popular *Dundee Courier, Evening Telegraph, Weekly News,* and *Weekly Welcome* are issued, occupies the important corner site, opposite Lamb's Hotel, long held by the old Post Office. The business of this most important government service is conducted within the splendid structure which we pass on the right as we near the boundary of the Howff. This old burying-ground is of quite exceptional interest. In fact, we may rank it among Scottish burial places as next to Greyfriars Cemetery, Edinburgh, in point of historic importance. Curiously enough, also, this Dundee cemetery was originally the grounds of the Greyfriars Monastery, which were granted to the town as a place of

THE BURNS STATUE.

THE ALBERT INSTITUTE—WEST SIDE.

THE ALBERT INSTITUTE—NORTH SIDE.

interment by Queen Mary in 1567. The Howff seemed to grow "fashionable" immediately, several of the fine monuments previously erected in the other Burgh kirkyards—St. Clement's, for instance, the site of which is now marked by the Town House—having been removed to the new cemetery, as their dates testify. Famous nobles of the shire, like Earl Beardie of Finhaven, lie buried here, with many generations of the city's higher and humbler population. Their memorials, where they exist, are, many of them, unique in design, decoration, and inscription, and are of such variety and note that several learned treatises have been written upon them. Their preservation is a public duty — their destruction, whether through ill-usage or neglect, pure vandalism. In the Old Steeple, the Howff, and the Cowgate Port Dundee possesses historical assets of priceless value, which are of national interest, and worthy of the tenderest care.

From Meadowside we enter Ward Road, with its numerous evidences of educational, religious, and social effort, and turn, almost

CLOCK TOWER, DUDHOPE CASTLE.

at a right angle, into a direct course for Lochee. On the left are
the extensive Tay Works of the Messrs Gilroy, and on the right
the Prison, and the Sheriff-court House, whose classic frontage
shows an elevation of singular dignity.   Next in order come
the Tramway Depot and the Power Station, a couple of important establishments in which the public do well to take the
deepest possible interest Soon the slopes of Dudhope meet
the view and sweeten the surroundings   These, for a consider-
able portion of the way, are mainly industrial, numbering
among them the great Carmichael iron foundry and engineering
works.   Of Dudhope Castle and Barracks, and the Barrack
Park during the time of the military occupation of the castle,
the older Dundonians have much to tell.   But the entire
property was acquired for the citizens by purchase from the
Earl of Home.   Dudhope Park is now a public playfield, the
Castle, Barracks, and Officers' quarters being devoted to purposes of recreation and instruction.   The landscape gardener
has transformed the bare slopes of other days into a veritable
garden, and Dudhope, with its shrubberies, flowers, and tree-
lined paths is a possession that any City might be proud to own.

It is interesting to recall the fact that the old castle of
Dudhope was the residence of the Scrymgeours, High Constables
of Dundee, and Heredi-
tary Bearers of the
Royal Standard of Scot-
land.   Graham of
Claverhouse, or "Bonnie
Dundee"—to give him
his lyric title — also
resided at Dudhope
during a part of his

WINDOW, DUDHOPE CASTLE.

dashing career, and others famous in their country's history
have found a home within its ancient walls.   It fell on evil

THE ROYAL EXCHANGE.

days when, towards the close of the 18th Century it was, for a couple of years, turned into a woollen mill! The Government of the time then acquired it as barracks, the castle being cruelly knocked about to fit it for usages somewhat germane to its original character. Now it appears as an **L** shaped building, with bold corner towers, and a turretted entrance, in which the old belfry is a picturesque detail. Dudhope is, withal, an interesting old structure, and its promenades, near one of which the Time Gun is placed, are as popular as they deserve to be.

OLD WELL, DUDHOPE PARK.

Soon we pass, on the left, the old estate and mansion of Logie, now in the builder's hands, and being covered with

DUDHOPE CASTLE.

streets and tenements. The ancient Kirkyard of Logie parish, with the ruined kirk—haunted and awful, if its local reputation is to be trusted—is a striking object on the left, before we turn into Lochee proper. A very direct road to the Law lies opposite the Parish Church of St. Thomas, which we have just passed, though Lochee people favour the approach by the Loons Road, on which they enter close by the railway station. It need scarcely be said that the Law deserves, and well repays a visit, whether approached from this quarter, from Inverlaw Place and the grounds of Dudhope House north of Dudhope Park, or from Constitution Road and Street. The latter route was the good old Dundee way of many a bygone year. Again we have the pleasure of remembering that this "grand auld hill" is also numbered among the splendid possessions of Dundee, and is, consequently, free to the public as is the invigorating air that blows around it. The views during the assent, and from the summit, which is over 600 feet high, are simply magnificent. There is little to circumscribe, nothing to intervene, unless, indeed, it be the great chimney of which Lochee is so inordinately vain. Even that very large and

LOOK OUT MAN.

ornate, though utilitarian adjunct of the Messrs Cox's enormous

works, looks at its best from this elevation, from which we can
see—as the look-out man puts it—"a' the warld and a bit o'
Fife."

The spreading tide of Tay—the pastoral richness of Strath
Dighty—the entire stretch of the swelling Sidlaws—all that,
and much more, rewards the toiler who has climbed the grassy
Law. And if he should note its contour carefully, or if he
ponder the meaning of many a mound and furrow, plain enough
to the "seeing eye," he may learn that here primæval or pre-
historic man erected the defences that he deemed strong
enough to defy not only his enemies but eternal time. Here
are the traces of the great ditch that ran round his fortress—
there the scanty indications of its fire-fused ramparts.
Hundreds could shelter within the strong enclosure that
crowned the Law : thousands might try to force them out, and
try in vain. It was one of Nature's fastnesses then, as now it
is one of her thrones, for here she is supreme, and her sway
supernal.

Lochee, perhaps, is not a place in which to linger, but
from the Car Terminus the Liff Road, and the Coupar-Angus
Road, lead directly to the open country, and to many pleasant
rural scenes. Camperdown House, the home of the descendants
of Dundee's distinguished son, Admiral, Lord Duncan, forms
to many the objective point of a ramble between cars. It
should be remembered that the great admiral did not live in
this fine classic mansion. It was built by his son, the first
Earl of Camperdown, who carefully gathered within the house
and grounds several interesting relics of his father's distinguished career. The Dundonian will recall, with pride, that
Provost Duncan of Dundee was the father of Lord Duncan,
and that the hero of Camperdown was born in Dundee in 1734.
Camperdown was originally known as Lundie. Its old castle
was Provost Duncan's country home, and the scene, it may be,

THE LAW FROM BALGAY HILL.

of the childhood of him who lived to cowe De Winter, the Dutch Terror of the Seas.

It may be well to remember that by Ancrum Road, a little south of Lochee Station, Balgay Hill is reached ; and by the South Lodge and Balgay Road the Blackness Road Section of the Tramway is available for a pleasant and varied return journey.

IV.—Maryfield and Forfar Road Section.

In olden days, the western end of the Murraygate, was as narrow as the Auld Brig o' Ayr, where, as Burns tells us, twa wheelbarrows trembled when they met.   In fact, the "Nairra o' the Morrygaet" became locally famous as a public nuisance, and was a positive danger prior to the improvements which made it possible to run the Tramway through this historic quarter.   The Murraygate, which we enter directly from the High Street, is now a typical city thoroughfare.   The newer buildings, like the British Linen Company's Bank on the right, and the extensive business premises opposite, indicate the march of progress, destined soon to bring the older portions of the Street into line with their resplendent neighbours

We leave the bustling Murraygate for the wider area of St. Andrew's Place, with its massive King's Theatre on the right, and on the left the calm dignity of the Cowgate Church.   The parish Church of St. Andrews, like the Town House, is of Adams' design, and is regarded as a good example of the work of these celebrated architects.

The Cowgate proper inclines slightly to the right of the Tramway Route, which at this point enters King Street. Almost its solitary ornament is the venerable Port spanning the narrow street, and just visible from the somewhat distant point of view.   It is worthy of closer inspection, however, for the

ST. ANDREW'S CHURCH.

ancient Cowgate Port is one of the most interesting and authentic of Dundee's antiquities. General Monk had some trouble with its defenders, who from the vanished parapet resisted his attacks ; and others, like Montrose, were made to feel the strength of its sturdy walls. In the time of pestilence, as tradition consistently affirms, George Wishart preached from its embattled crest to those in quarantine without the walls, and in many other historic Dundee scenes the East Port played a gallant part. It was thoroughly restored in 1877, and embellished with an inscription, indicative of its history and importance, which the visitor should study.

King Street, a well-built residential thoroughfare, merges in Princes Sreet, which is dominated by the enormous bulk of the Baxter Mills. This extensive enterprise gives a lead to the distinctive industry of "Juteopolis," the various works covering an area of nine acres, and giving employment to some 4000 people. The Arbroath Road extension of the Tramway service diverges to the right at the top of Princes Street, leading to the Baxter Park and the Eastern Necropolis, which will, in due course, come under notice.

The route is continued by Albert Street, till, at the parting of the ways, the magnificent Morgan Academy commands the widening view. The pedestrian should note that Mains Loan, the street to the left just beyond the U.F. Church, leads directly to the Castle and Den of Mains, the Pitkerro Road to the right of the Morgan Grounds, leading to the northern entrance of the Baxter Park. The Academy, now a flourishing and popular Secondary School, was originally known as the Morgan Hospital. It was built and endowed by the benefaction of a wealthy Indian merchant, Mr John Morgan, who took this means of showing his interest in his native town. Hundreds of boys—many of them bearing the favoured name of the founder—were boarded and educated at "The Morgan" during

THE OLD EAST PORT.

its earlier years. But the character of the Institution was completely changed by the action of the Endowed Schools Commissioners. Now, the bursary system is in the ascendant, and education is the only business conducted within the stately pile. Its architectural effect is singularly good ; and it may be at once conceded that the Scottish Baronial style was never more happily adapted to educational requirements than in this grand example designed by Messrs Peddie and Kinnear.

From the Academy to the Terminus, the route passes through an entensive and beautiful villa district, Stobs Muir Reservoir and Skating Ponds appearing on the right. Beyond the Terminus lies the open country, the Forfar Road descending gradually to the Vale of Dighty, and rising over Powrie Brae, on whose broad shoulder is seen entrenched the old Castle of Powrie, the ancient and picturesque home of the powerful Fotheringhams. This is the favourite road to Mains Castle and Den, Dighty Bridge marking the turning to the left that leads to the favourite resort. Claverhouse and Baldovan form an extension of the ramble westwards, and the return journey can be made by way of the Cars at Downfield or Fairmuir. There is nothing finer in its way among the surroundings of Dundee than this lovely road by the classic Dighty, and a leisure afternoon is well spent in making acquaintance with its varied delights.

The village of Claverhouse, near the Bleach Works, comes as a revelation to the explorer, so quaintly rural is it, and so effectively set amid the verdure of the well-watered valley. The Dovecot, too, is more than merely pictorial. If the traditional "oldest inhabitant" is to be trusted, this unique structure not only marks the site of old Claver House, but is built of its very stones ! It may thus be regarded as a striking memorial of John Graham, who here first saw the light of day ; and may, at a pinch, be taken to symbolise the dove-like nature

THE MORGAN ACADEMY.

THE DOVECOT AT CLAVERHOUSE.

of his disposition, which certain of his biographers stoutly affirm and maintain.

The Parish Church of Mains and Strathmartine may also tempt a short digression, for its churchyard is full of interest to all to whom the annals of the district may have a voice. Still further westwards, Baldovan enchants the eye, so sweetly rural is the primitive old village, and yet so near the town. Finer subjects for pencil, brush, or camera, are nowhere to be found than in these charming old cottages whose white walls, with tiled or thatched roofs, smile from the luscious background of Baldovan woods. But the charms of the Dighty are not amenable to such hurried notes as these, they must be seen to be appreciated at their true value ; but, once enjoyed, they will retain the full allegiance of every leal wayfarer.

For generations the Den of Mains has been a favourite resort of the Dundee holiday maker, and still it charms both old and young to revel by the Gelly Burn. The Castle lifts its lofty tower over the verdant howes, telling of the lordly

CASTLE OF MAINS, OR FINTRY.

Grahames who built it in the 16th century, and called it
Fintry, as the records of their
warlike race avow. Good
builders they were in the
stirring days of old : no need
to go further than to Fintry to
prove what few will care to con-
trovert. Much of the original
structure remains, joined to
those more modern and less
romantic appendages that
mark its ancient form. The
tall, narrow tower, with its
pent-house roof ; the turrets,
tablets, and mouldings of the
crumbling walls ; the arched

WINDOW IN MAINS CASTLE.

entrance, the balcony, the corbelling, and the corbie steps,
combine to make of Fintry one of the most picturesque of
Scottish ruins. It was no great stronghold like the Castle of
Broughty ; but simply a strongly built, well defended, and
somewhat ornamental example of a fortified Scottish mansion,
and as such is interesting to architects, as its story is to
archæologists, and its venerable beauty is to all.

Tradition has it that the well of the ancient Church of
Mains—just over the Gelly Burn from the Castle—was the
scene of the tragedy of the Nine Maidens, whose fate gave to
so many of our Scottish springs their sympathetic appellation.
Here the nine sisters came, and here they perished one by one,
as runs the ancient story. And from the "Sinavey" Well
their avenger pursued the monster who destroyed them till it
fell beneath the frenzied blows he dealt it from "Strickmartin"
to "Baldraigon." The Ninewells of Invergowrie, Forfar,
Glamis, and many other places all over Scotland, keep green

the memory of the hapless maidens of Pitempton ; and, should
any scoffer doubt the story of their tragic fate, is not the
monster graven on many an ancient stone whose meaning the
legend alone can unravel ?

OLD STAIRWAY IN TOWER, MAINS CASTLE.

THE TAY BRIDGE, FROM BLACKNESS ROAD TERMINUS.

V.—Blackness and Balgay Section.

This short but important route follows the Nethergate and Perth Road lines, till, opposite St. Andrew's R.C. Church, it turns sharply into South Tay Street. This favourite residential quarter has not escaped the notice of the local humourist, who has dubbed it "Pill Raw," a sort of left handed compliment to the medical profession, many of whom reside in Tay Street. The West Port is soon reached, and we note, in passing, that however historical or important this ancient gateway may have been. it had not the slightest connection with the West Port of "Bonnie Dundee," which the context of that ballad clearly shows to have been the *Edinburgh* gate of the same designation.

The Brook Street district—of old the Scouringburn—and the nearer portions of the Blackness Road, give many indications of the enormous population confined within their narrow bounds. But, with every turning of the way, the prospect widens and brightens, and it is a relief to think how easy it is to escape for an hour or two from the congestion of the neighbourhood. There are, comparatively, few objects of interest on the way. The Blackness Foundry, and the Liff and Benvie Poorhouse are passed on the right; St. Joseph's Church and Convent, and the old mansion of Blackness on the left. The Blackness estate like others that we have seen, has been handed over to the speculative builder, who is rapidly covering its sloping grounds with streets of villas and superior tenement dwellings. The situation is choice, and the surroundings beautiful. It is surprising, almost, to find such salubrity of residence within a few minutes run from the heart of the city.

A short distance beyond the Terminus at Balgay Road is the new entrance to the Victoria Hospital, interesting to all because of its mission of mercy to incurables, and specially interesting to those older Dundonians who knew the central portion of old as Balgay House, the residence of Harry Scott, once prominent in the City's Parliamentary affairs. On the crest of the ground just beyond the Hospital entrance, is the Industrial School for Girls, a very fine building, designed on characteristically Scottish lines by MacLaren & Sons of Dundee. Its massive central block is reminiscent of Dudhope, and with its beautiful grounds and wide surroundings, this effective modern structure might be ranked as a model for Institutions of its class. The views over Tay, from its terraced front, are splendid, the great viaduct appearing very impressive from this coign of vantage

We skirt Victoria Park, a useful public playfield, *en route* for Balgay, on which we enter by the charming Lodge, and a delightful avenue lined with foliage and blossom. Alternating with the shrubs and flowers, are several relics of old Dundee, including pinnacles and graven stones, brought here after the restoration of the Old Steeple, and useful even in their decay. From the main pathway several narrower paths give access to the upper reaches of the Hill, and even there we shall find various carved and cusped memorials of St. Mary's Tower grouped here and there in admirable disorder. Near the centre of the promenade a capacious Pavilion offers rest and shelter; and just at this point the noble Hill assumes its most picturesque aspect. A deep and wide gorge seems to cut it into two sections, which are spanned by an arch of singular elegance. The pathways that traverse the higher levels are continued over this handsome iron structure, which blends so harmoniously with its surroundings of rock and tree as to form an almost perfect picture. But Balgay is simply a succession of pictures; and whether the outlook be *from* the Hill towards the wider prospects, or *to* the Hill itself, with its wealth of woodland

North Lodge.

South Lodge.

"BONNIE BALGAY."

scenery, the results are invariably inspiring, and altogether delightful.

Part of the western area of the Hill, with the lower contiguous grounds, form the beautiful Cemetery known as the Western Necropolis. In the south-east angle of this picturesque "God's acre," and close to the bridge that spans the deep ravine, lies all that is mortal of the great George Gilfillan. His monument, of stalwart form and size, seems no unworthy emblem of the massive intellect and manly character of the great poet, preacher, and critic. Assuredly, it is well to remember to pay this sacred spot a visit, for here, with many of

GILFILLAN MONUMENT.

his humbler contemporaries, lies he whose like we may never see again.

The views of Tay, of the Carse of Gowrie, and, notably, of Lochee and the Law, are well worthy of the exertion requisite in order to reach the higher vantages of Balgay. But the visitor, in his anxiety to embrace the wider horizon, should not forget to note his immediate surroundings, for nature has been lavish of her gifts in the adornment of this grand public pleasance. The extent of the ground is wonderful ; the expanse of its vistas, and the variety of their foliation delighting the rambler who lingers long enough to explore the many nooks and pathways of the fair demesne. Here he will find a woodland scene such as England might fail to rival, and there he will mark a rocky scaur that might fill with envy the genius of a Highland Glen. There is peace on Balgay, also, as well as beauty ; and there is balm in every wandering breeze that carols through its vernal bowers.

RELICS OF ST. MARY'S TOWER.

From the western shoulder of the Hill, the visitor will be able to note, and to reach, the route leading southwards by Glamis Road to the Cars on the Perth Road Section. Another alternative route homewards may be seen and reached from the eastern portion of the Hill. This leads by the North, or Dalhousie Gate, round the Lochee Park—the gift of Cox Brothers —and by Ancrum Road to the Cars on the Lochee Section. It need scarcely be said that the variety offered by such alternations of route as these, adds immensely to the pleasure of an outing ; and the Balgay Hill Circular Tour, if so we may term it, may be heartily recommended as an experiment to all on pleasure bent.

IN BALGAY PARK   "WHERE SHADOWS FALL."

VI.—The Arbroath Road Section.

As was indicated previously, this short line leaves the Forfar Road Section at the head of Princes Street. From there it runs due east, serves a very important district, and is the popular route for the Baxter Park. Beyond the Terminus lie the High School Recreation Grounds, and the Eastern Necropolis. A pleasant and favourite circular journey can be effected by walking from the Park entrance, or Dalkeith Road, to the gateway of the Necropolis, and thence south by Dalgleish Road to Craigie Terrace Terminus on the Broughty Ferry route. The Park and the Necropolis may thus be visited on the way, or the Park can be negotiated from the northern entrance in Pitkerro Road, the remainder of the ramble following the directions otherwise.

The Eastern Necropolis is regarded as chief among the Cemeteries of the City, both in point of extent and beauty. Its area corresponds to that of the Baxter Park ; but the silent city of the dead, however beautiful in its adornments, can enter into no competition with the glowing garden of the living. This was the first of Dundee's Public Parks, and holds its own for spacious elegance among its more recent compeers. For these magnificent pleasure and recreation grounds, Dundee is for ever indebted to the late Sir David Baxter, and his sisters, the Misses Baxter, a trio of benefactors who thus, and in other ways, have earned the encomiums of the citizens of every degree.

The grounds and pathways were disposed and planned by Sir Joseph Paxton, and are kept in perpetual order by an endowment made by the donors. The large southern area remains open as a sporting field, the remainder forming a delightful garden, intersected with winding walks, and gay with flowers

THE PAVILION, BAXTER PARK.

and foliage. From the Flagstaff on the highest point of the ground the prospects are charming. The broad central promenade, the beautiful Pavilion, the Rock Garden, the Lodges, everything of comfort, beauty, pleasure, or instruction seems perfect in its appointments. Assuredly, the Baxter Park is an enormous boon to a City like Dundee, and it is gratifying to find the citizens making use so largely of its benefits.

VII.—Fairmuir and Constitution Road Section.

This important Section is served by cars of a special type —'single deckers,' they may be termed—necessary on account of the remarkably stiff gradients encountered on the way. From Reform Street we follow the Lochee route for a short distance. leaving it at the Post Office to find Constitution Road rising steep and straight before us. Half a century ago, the braeside which we are to traverse was guiltless of stone and lime. Constitution Road was but a hedge-bordered country lane leading to the Law, which then, as now, formed the objective of as healthful a "constitutional" as may anywhere be found.

The new General Post Office, an effective and elaborate building, is admirably equipped for the great and growing Postal Service of the city. Perhaps no better indication could be given of the progress and position of Dundee than the unceasing whirl of business transacted within these handsome walls. Ward Chapel, on the left, is representative of the ideals held by the Congregationalists in Dundee, this elegant Gothic structure having a long and honourable history as the leading local church of the denomination. The premises of the Y.M.C.A , and of the Dundee Savings Bank, are also worthy of notice among the more important buildings of the locality.

The New Cemetery, whose old name now sounds rather

archaic, is used only as an open space and promenade. Its quiet retirement is grateful to those who care to muse upon the past, which here is represented by several quaint inscriptions and sculptures. The long elevation of the Volunteer Drill Hall is seen on the west of the ground ; Chapelshade Parish Church, and the Unitarian Church overlooking it from the east. Indeed, churches are numerous in this quarter, but the upper levels of the hill, with the Bleaching Green, and the villa-lined Terraces, are upon us ere we have time to observe them all The "greens" have long been popular as a washing and bleaching ground, and even in these days of steam laundries their advantages are not forgotten. The time was when the Meadow Burn, or St. Francis' Well, watered half the washings of Dundee, left out of nights under the charge of watchmen, who were paid a small fee for their vigilance.

Noblest among the public buildings of Dundee, both for situation and purpose, is the Royal Infirmary, round whose frontages to south, west, and north, we are now travelling. It crests the Dudhope braes in a manner truly coronal, and forms an excellent example of the successful adaptation of structure and site. Its architects, Messrs Coe & Goodwin of London, adopted in its design a free treatment of the Tudor style, and secured a measure of grace and cheerfulness by vari-coloured masonry, a picturesque elevation, and a freedom of lighting that is pleasing without and within. The Institution has for long proved a blessing to the City and district, as is amply attested by its popularity among all classes, and by the bene- factions that have within recent years doubled its extent and usefulness.

The building has a southern frontage of 350 feet, this great mass being divided into a boldly advanced central pavilion, showing octagonal corner towers, the wings being relieved by gabled projections, knit by bold string courses, and

THE ROYAL INFIRMARY.

ornamented with fine oriels.   Undoubtedly, the Infirmary has
an appearance more English than Scottish, but there is a charm
in variety, and the newer buildings on the north accentuate
that truism.   These include the splendid Cancer and Maternity
Hospitals, erected and endowed by J. K. Caird, LL.D., a range
of ornate buildings that seem to translate us suddenly from
Dudhope to mediæval Nuremburg.   The Nurses' Home, also
distinctive in style was largely the gift of Sir W. O. Dalgleish.
To the original endowment of Miss Soutar, many donors have
added, here a little there a little, till now the Infirmary seems
to be as complete as wealth and skill can make it.   As an
Institution it is splendidly managed ; and the highest medical
skill of the City is here at the service of the humblest citizen
requiring it.

We have passed the eastern entrance into Dudhope Park,
rounded the Infirmary, and have reached Somerville Place and
the top of Constitution Road.   As has been indicated, the
favourite road to the Law is from this point, the way lying by
Upper Constitution Street and the High U.F. Church.   Rosebank Church appears on the right, in Constitution Street ; and
on the left, in Rosebank Street, is the Empire Music Hall.
The locality grows denser as we proceed, turning northwards
into Hilltown, which has the distinction of being the steepest
street in Dundee, a fact that means more than mere words
seem to convey.   Of old, the Hilltown was known as the
Bonnethill, a name that still trips on the tongues of the older
race of Dundonians.   The manufacture of men's bonnets was
plied briskly within the cottages on the Hill, and for many
generations these "Bonnets o' Bonnie Dundee" had a reputation as great as Kilmarnock nightcaps ever had.   They were a
self-contained, independent, and unruly set, these "Hill Tribes"
of the bonnet industry.   They met and mauled their lowlier
neighbours in many a sanguinary scrimmage, and from their

Hill fastnesses defied the authority of even the Provost and Magistrates of Dundee. In fact, we have nothing in our local lore to match these oft-recurring encounters, except the celebrated quarrels between the souters and weavers of Forfar and Kirriemuir. Truth to tell, the "Rotten Raw" militants often had the upper hand of their antagonists, for, as Evan Dhu says in "Waverley," "Even a haggis, God bless her, can charge down a hill!"

The bonnet trade flourished, declined, and fell into decay, which was relieved by the advent of the handloom. That, in turn, has disappeared, and the rattle of the factory shuttle is eloquent of the staple trade of the locality. Main Street, a little further on, shows a Car Terminus useful for those who desire to make an "inner circle" run embracing almost all the "Hill country," and leading to or from the city by either of the routes to Fairmuir and Downfield. But we speed on our way thither, passing the useful Pillar Clock, presented to the district by Lord Provost Barrie, and noting to left and right a couple of the admirable Board Schools with which the city is studded. At Coldside the lines of both the Fairmuir routes converge, the track still leading by the Strathmartine Road to Downfield Station. The Fair Muir, another name redolent of ancient usages, is now a public Recreation Ground, gifted to the City by Sir John Ogilvy, M.P., of Baldovan, a public spirited gentleman and landowner, whose memory as a benefactor will long be cherished.

The Fairmuir here introduces us to the large and important suburb of Downfield, almost entirely occupied by beautiful villa residences. Some of the recently erected houses, notably those designed by Mr Charles G. Soutar, are delightful evidences of the desire for art in the dwelling, of which so much is heard in these times. Downfield has lately been incorporated within the boundary of the city, and now enjoys

BALDOVAN VILLAGE.

the benefits of an extended Tramway Service. This shortens
the ramble by Baldovan, Mains, and Forfar Road, already
described, and opens out to the visitor the charms of a district
not too well known by city people. There is a delightful walk
by the side of the Gelly Burn right on to the Den of Mains,
and Lochee can be reached by rail, or by ways more devious
and rural. Several fine Church buildings, and the Industrial
School for boys, are noticeable features in a neighbourhood
that can boast with good reason of its salubrity and beauty.

VIII.—The Fairmuir Section.

This route avoids the zig-zags and heavy gradients of the
Constitution Road Section, and serves the populous districts
opening off Victoria Road, and lying near the Dens Road.
The Cars start from Commercial Street, a galaxy of magnificent
business premises, showing many of the finest shops in the city,
and worthy in its style and importance of even a metropolitan
reputation. Keiller's celebrated confectionery works are hidden
from sight on the left; the eastern portion of the Albert
Institute, known as the Victoria Galleries appears before us;
and soon we are passing the handsome square to take the
sweeping turn that leads into Victoria Road, of old the Buckle-
maker Wynd.

Just before leaving Albert Square, we note on the left the
Royal Exchange, one of the finest buildings in the city. This
palace of commerce, for so it may justly be termed, was a
pioneer among the elegant structures of the neighbourhood.
Great difficulties were encountered in securing a solid founda-
tion in the marshy ground of the site, and David Bryce's
masterpiece appears to-day shorn of its crown, and somewhat
faulty in its lines, on that account. The tower, particularly,
was affected through the sinking of the sub-structure, and it

was decided, judiciously, to abandon the beautiful spire which might have proved a burden impossible for it to carry. But the Exchange, even as we see it, in the rich exuberance of its Flemish architecture, is worthy of the Albert Square, and of the important transactions conducted within, or outside its walls.

Victoria Road introduces us to a remarkable variety of buildings ; central offices for some of the great manufacturers of the city, Insurance Offices, Calender Works, the Gaiety Theatre, Churches, Schools, and residential tenements innumerable. Near Victoria Bridge, where the lines take a northward turning, an excellent idea may be formed of the enormous extent of the Dens Works, owned by the Messrs Baxter. Their tall, pointed chimneys, look like mighty Egyptian Obelisks, and dominate the local views, which are of a strictly utilitarian aspect. The desigination of Dens Road reminds us of the time when the grassy banks of the Dens Burn, now submerged under a wilderness of stone and lime, were gay with wild flowers, and merry with the laughter of youth that paidled there "·frae mornin' sun till dine." Intermittently, in the spaces between the great mills and factories that line the route, glimpses may be caught of its pristine condition, but the Den is now a centre of industry, and its beauties but a memory !

The Main Street lines, already noticed, diverge sharply westwards about the middle of Dens Road. The grounds of the Dundee Football Club, known as Dens Park, are seen to the right, Moncur Crescent leading through the feuing ground of West Clepington to the junction of the lines at Coldside. Here the new Branch Public Library is now completed and augurs well for the success of the Carnegie gifts. The old mansion house looks sadly through its screen of " tall ancestrial trees " on a network of projected streets that soon may cover its verdant surroundings. There is a touch of pathos in the

thought that these fine old estates are being committed to the
tender mercies of the builder ; but sentiment is at a discount
when a great city must perforce take wings, and spread itself
afield.   The Fair Muir gives a name to another large residential
portion of the neighbourhood, westwards of which lies the
splendid buildings of King's Cross Fever Hospital, another of
Dundee's important remedial Institutions   The Clepington
Road, here skirting the estates of the same name, and the Fairmuir houses, leads to the Forfar Road, and offers the option of
a walk between the sections, shorter than that by Downfield,
Baldovan and Mains, though the rambler will miss the charms
of the limpid Dighty ; or the Road can now be negotiated by
means of the newly built Trackless Trolley line connecting
Fairmuir with Maryfield, and linking up these two routes.
This is referred to more at length under No. IX.   From the
junction of the lines at Coldside, Loons Road indicates a variant
route that leads westwards to Lochee.   Both roads, to east or
west, cover a distance of "a mile and a bittock," that to the
west leading through the open country, till on crossing the
Dundee and Newtyle Railway it merges in Harefield Road,
from which the Terminus, or the High Street of Lochee are
easily negotiable.

IX.—Trackless Trolley Line, Maryfield to Fairmuir.

One somewhat unsatisfactory feature of Dundee Tramway
system, from the management point of view, is the fact that
while all the lines radiate directly from the centre of the city,
they all terminate in loose ends, and no provision has, up till
recently, been possible by way of a circular tour.   One reason
for this, of course, lies in the heavy cost of permanent way
entailing charges outwith profitable running in more sparsely
populated districts.   As a result, attention has for some years

been directed to a trackless system which has obtained some vogue on the Continent. A Committee visited Germany to investigate the matter, but its labours have only materialized within the last few months, when the first Trackless Trolley System in Scotland has been installed in the northern part of the city. This experimental section which, as part of a completed scheme, might lead to the encircling of the city in this way, links up the important residential district of Maryfield with the Fairmuir and Downfield Starting from Stobsmuir Reservoir it traverses the Clepington Road in its entire length of $1\frac{1}{4}$ miles. Passing on the south the grounds of the Eastern Hospital and Poorhouse, we soon have on our right the important chair factory of F. East & Co. While extensive tenement blocks frequently obscure the view, the passenger cannot fail to be charmed with the magnificent vista of hill and vale to the north. Over the bed of the Dighty, with Mains Castle in the near distance, one is faced by the rapid rise to the Emmock crowned ridge, backed in the further distance by the more massive slopes of the Sidlaws. To the south a bird's-eye view of the city — impossible from almost any other point—can be obtained, merging in the noble sweep of the Tay, with the nearer Hills of Fife. On a clear day the spires of St. Andrews can be descried beyond these, and altogether no finer view of Dundee and its surroundings can be obtained than by a journey on this route. The massive shoulder of the Law is turned to us as we bowl along the macadam roadway. Soon we run into industrial quarters again with Victoria Foundry and Dundee Carpet Works, indicating our near approach to the Strathmartine Road and King's Cross Hospital, near which the trackless system reaches its present terminus.

While an experiment, its promoters hope that its success may lead to a wider extension of the system in the interests of tramway patrons and the public at large. Certainly no better route could have been chosen for experimental purposes, either from a utilitarian or an æsthetic point of view.

In Conclusion.

And so our journeys together are done. If the somewhat discursive remarks of the present writer have added any interest to these travels the object of this work has not been altogether unfulfilled. And, I think, you will agree that, despite the disadvantages under which such an ancient city may labour in modernizing itself, and conforming to the standards (public health, social and æsthetic) of modern days, Dundee has not altogether failed to rise to the height of her opportunities, and to benefit from her incomparable natural situation.

ST. PETER'S CHURCH, PERTH ROAD

THE SCENE OF M'CHEYNE'S MINISTRY.

PETER FISHER, GENERAL MANAGER AND ENGINEER.

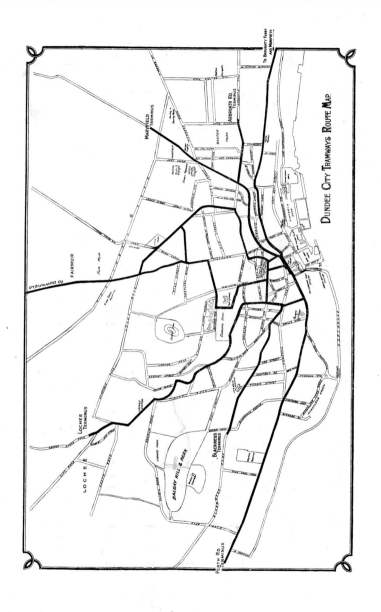

DUNDEE CITY TRAMWAYS ROUTE MAP.

TO BROUGHTY FERRY AND MONIFIETH

ARBROATH RD. TERMINUS

MARYFIELD TERMINUS

TO DOWNFIELD

FAIRMUIR

LOCHEE TERMINUS

LOCHEE

BALGAY HILL & PARK

LOCHEE PARK

BLACKNESS TERMINUS

PERTH RD. TERMINUS

FARES.

On all Sections, WHOLE DISTANCE
to and from High Street, Dundee **1d.**

HALFPENNY STAGES.

PERTH ROAD SECTION.

High Street and Ellenbank, ...	Either Way.
Ellenbank and Step Row, ...	,,
Step Row and Rockfield, ...	,,
Windsor Street and West Park, ...	,,
Rockfield and Farington Street, ...	,,
Farrington Terrace and Ninewells, ...	,,

MARYFIELD SECTION.

High Street and Crescent Street, ...	Either Way.
Crescent Street and Stobswell, ...	,,
Stobswell and Maryfield, ...	,,

FERRY ROAD SECTION.

High Street and Middle Street, ...	Either Way.
Middle Street and Thornbank, ...	,,
Thornbank and Dalgleish Road, ...	,,
Taybank and Craigie Terrace Tramway Station, ...	,,

BAXTER PARK SECTION.

High Street and Crescent Street, ...	Either Way.
Crescent Street and Baxter Park West Gate, ...	,,
Top of Princes Street and Dalkeith Road, ...	,,
Craig Pier and Foot of Wellgate, ...	

LOCHEE SECTION.

High Street and Dudhope Crescent Road, ...   Either Way.
Dudhope Crescent Road and Polepark, ...   ,,
Polepark and Coupar Street, ...   ,,
Coupar Street and High Street, Lochee, Tramway Station,   ,,
Loons Road and Lochee Terminus, ...   ,,

BLACKNESS SECTION.

High Street and West Port Tramway Station,   ...   Either Way.
West Port Tramway Station and Ure Street,   ...   ,,
Ure Street and Balgay Lodge, ...   ,,

CONSTITUTION ROAD SECTION.

High Street and Barrack Road Tramway Station, ...   Either Way.
Barrack Road Tramway Station and Constitution Street,   ,,
Top of Barrack Road and Top of Main Street,   ...   ,,

FAIRMUIR AND DOWNFIELD SECTION.

High Street and Nelson Street, ...   Either Way.
Nelson Street and Hillbank, ...   ,,
Hillbank and Top of Moncur Crescent, ...   ,,
Dura Street and Top of Main Street, ...   ,,
Hill Street School and Clepington Road, ...   ,,
Top of Moncur Crescent and Fairmuir Tramway Station,   ,,
Fairmuir Tramway Station and Gellyburn,   ...   ,,
Sherbrook Street and Baldovan Road, ...   ,,

CHILDREN and YOUNG PERSONS between 2 years of age and 14 years of age any distance to or from High Street, Dundee, $\frac{1}{2}$d.